W9-CQJ-657

# WORKING PLACES

For Tom Dunne

# WORKING PLACES

## by Jeffrey Weiss
## Photography by David Leach

Additional photography by Michael Kanouff, Jon Elliot and Jeffrey Weiss

St. Martin's Press
New York

Copyright © 1980 by Jeffrey Weiss

All rights reserved. For information, write:
St. Martin's Press, Inc., 175 Fifth Avenue, New York, N.Y. 10010.

Manufactured in the United States of America

Library of Congress Cataloging in Publication Data

Weiss, Jeffrey.
 Working Places.

 1. Work environment—Pictorial works.  2. In-
terior decoration—Pictorial works.  3. Office
layout—Pictorial works.  I. Title.

HF5547.F74   747'.852   79-27160

ISBN 0-312-88984-4

ISBN 0-312-88985-2 pbk.

## Acknowledgements

Antenna Enterprises, New York City. Designed by Jason Croy and David Browne.

Bank of Eureka Springs, John Cross—Presi-
dent.

Ninepatch A Quilt Store and More, Elaine
Zelnick—owner, Lissa Van Duyts—manager,
Berkeley, California.

William Kirsch, Architect. Sausalito, California.

Degn Greer.

Donald Soloman M.D. and Nan Kohler M.S.
Sebastapol, California. Designed and built by
Richard Eichenholz, Sebastapol, California.

Lori Hanson, Berkeley, California. Fence
designed and built by Paul Minault, Berkeley,
California.

Ivan and Marilyn Karp. Design by Marilyn
Gelfman-Pereira.

Dean and Deluca, East Hampton. Designed
by Jack Ceglic.

Bea Lopez Handmade Paper Art Cards,
Berkeley, California.

Vincent Trocchia, Architect. New York City.

Marta MacDonald.

Gary Camardo and Amanda DuBack, Three
Wishes Shop, West Broadway, New York.
Building design by Charles DuBack.

Hamilton Chiropractic offices. Architect: War-
ren C. Fuller, Oakland, California.

Tender Buttons, New York City.

Imprints, New York City. Martin Greene.

Paramount Theater, Oakland, California.
Peter Botto—manager.

Stan Herman Design Studio, New York City.

Design: Carl Berkowitz.

Production: Color Book Design, Inc., Barbara
Frontera.

# Contents

READING ROOM

If only I had the proper desk, I have often thought, then all my thwarted ambitions to write a great novel would immediately come to fruition. Friends speak to me, sometimes wistfully, of the office, shop, bank or studio they have designed in their minds' eye—a place of perfect beauty coupled with a utility that makes work flow effortlessly. Many times those disembodied yearnings for the perfect working place are far less difficult to make actual than at first seems apparent. What is required, of course, is a certain amount of space, some money and in some cases here illustrated, a great deal of money and perhaps most important, a sure notion of what you want.

One of the most spectactular and successful stores in the resort area of East Hampton is Dean and Deluca. The proprietors wanted a feeling that maintained the basic integrity of the original architecture. The intense visual excitement of their store is a product of the combined effect of the bare walls and the planned traffic flow through central display islands. In fact, the display is a response to the exhibition and presentation needs of their merchandise. Cheese, pastry, pate, kitchenware all have their own "framed" space. They seem to float on a gleaming chrome-framed glass canvas. While the front of the cases resembles the great food stalls at Harrod's in London, the streamed yet overwhelmingly appetizing displays of choice foods is a dynamic, uncliched and successful visual and

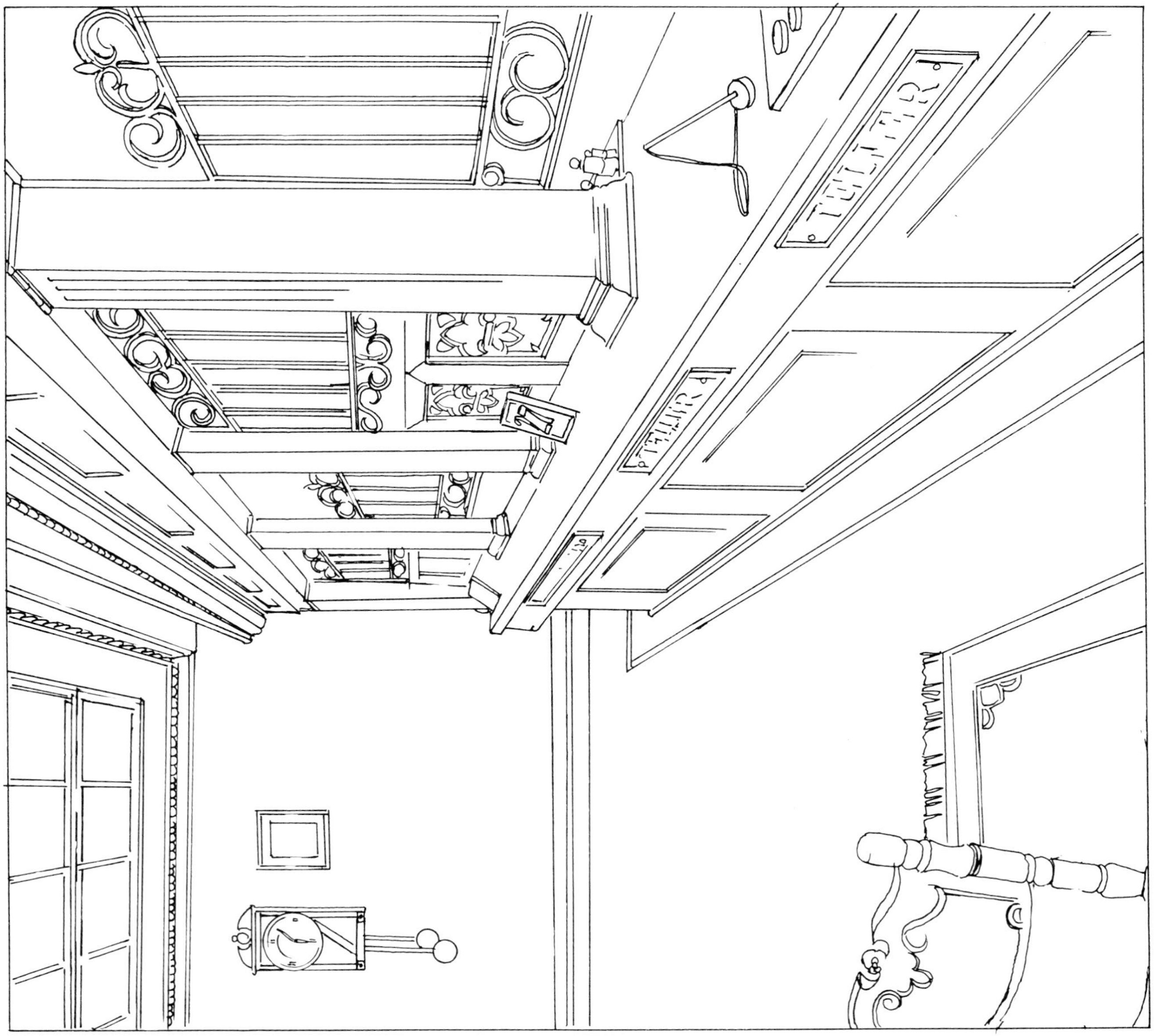

BANK

commercial achievement.

At the Bank of Eureka Springs an opposite sensibility comes into play. One of the most charming and picturesque towns in the South, Eureka Springs is a treasure-trove of period architecture. The intentionally quaint and old fashioned treatment of the Bank not only is in keeping with the physical character of the town but reflects its temperament as well. A more secure place to trust your money to would be hard to imagine.

The same attention to style of place is true of Peter Botto's office at the Paramount theater. Built as a movie and vaudeville house in 1931 it is now a showcase for the performing arts. But the flair of the manager's office is maintained in the original art deco collection, the period paintings from the studio of Anthony Heinzberger, the design consultant who was overseer for the theater's restoration and the whimsy of Botto's own 300 member pig collection. The design of the office fully reflects the spirit of the theater, what Peter Botto calls the "nifty deco look."

At Antenna—the hair-cutting establishment, the work space was modified to reflect the owner's belief that conventional salons were uncomfortable to both workers and patrons coupled with the desire to maintain the spacious studio of Louis Tiffany, Antenna utilizes the sheer space available and a fantastic sound system to insure the privacy of the stylist and the client. Gone is the need for

ARTISTS STUDIO

cubicles or partitions, moreover a constantly changing display of art and flowers renews the space.

The weaver's studio reflects another kind of ambiance, one geared to the private needs and utilitarian concerns of the artisan: Here as in the studio of a stained glass maker and fabric artist necessity has been joined with the artist's eye to create working places of ingenious beauty. Materials, tools, even the jumble of a desk or the bulletin board reflect a concern with color and line.

In the many other special spaces in **Working Places,** the same ability to transform the ordinary into the delightful is at work.

In my work I depend on the good will and help of dozens of people. The owners and designers of the places shown were generous in showing their ideas. In addition, I am grateful to those who helped with leads and suggestions, particularly Stewart and Maryann Teacher, Erin Clermont, Bob Ubell and Rosalyn Deutche. My friends at St. Martin's Press, Ashton Applewhite and Tim McGuire were terrific as were my production team—Walter Berkower, Dan and Richard Sirota, Barbara Frontera and Allan Blumenthal. And yet again Yolande got me through.

Jeffrey Weiss
Sag Harbor, 1980

ARCHITECTS

FOOD STORE

A Haircutters

# A Country Bank

A Quilt Store & More

# An Architect

# A Stained Glass Artist

A Gynecologist

A Textile Artist

# An Art Dealer & An Artist

A Food Store

# A Fiber Artist

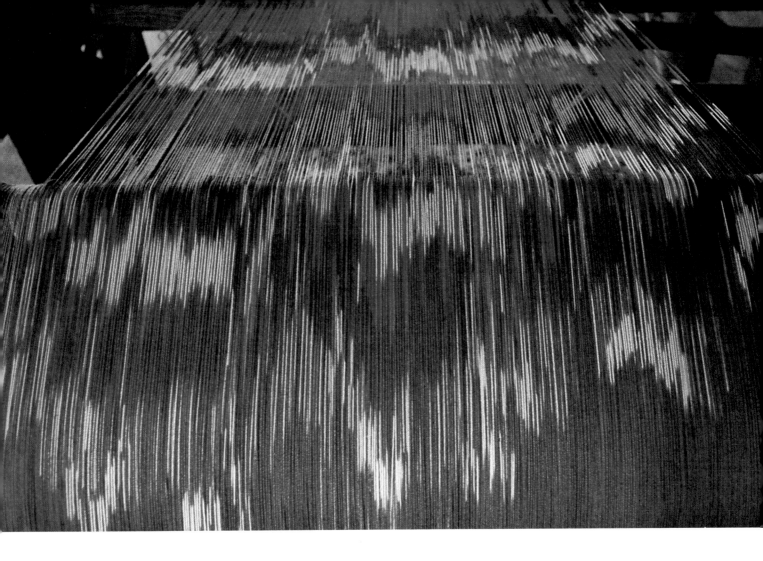

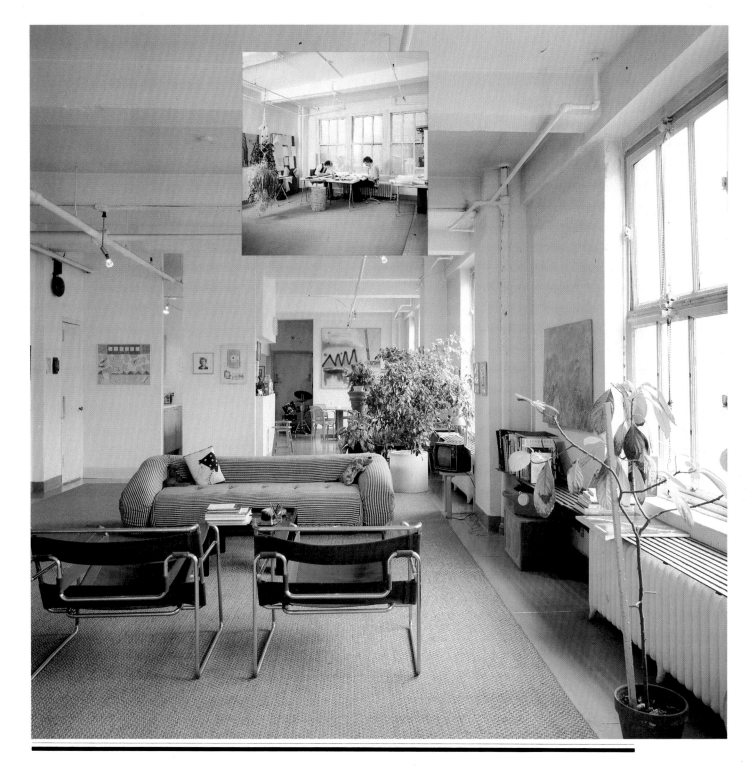

# An Architect

# A Weaver

# A Dress Shop & Design Studio

## A Natural Healer

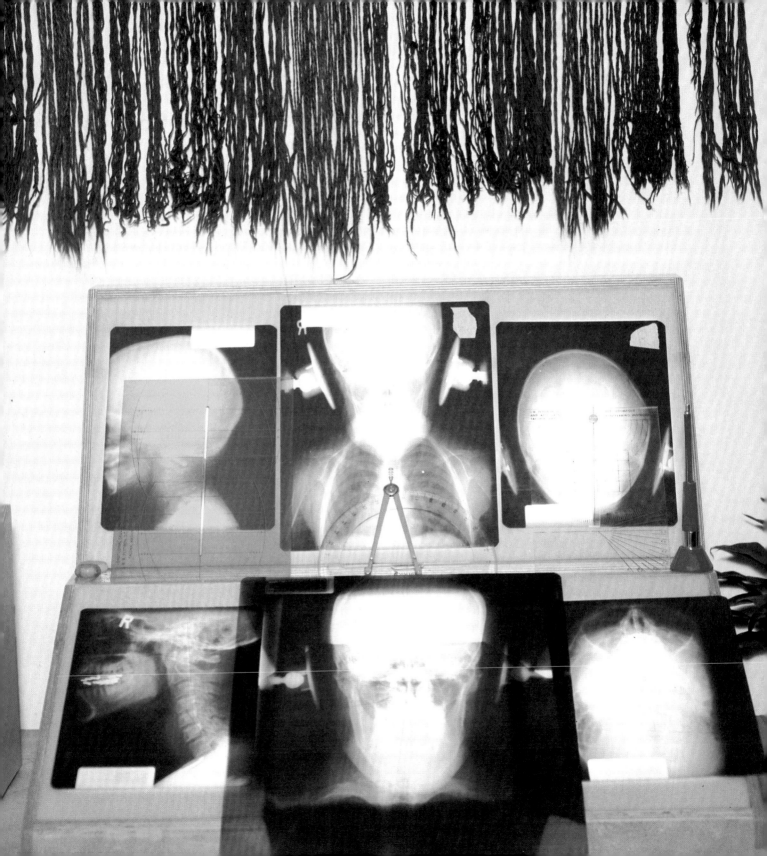

# A Weaver

A Button Shop

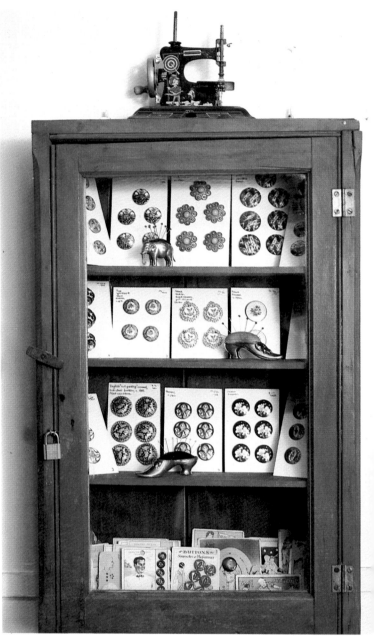

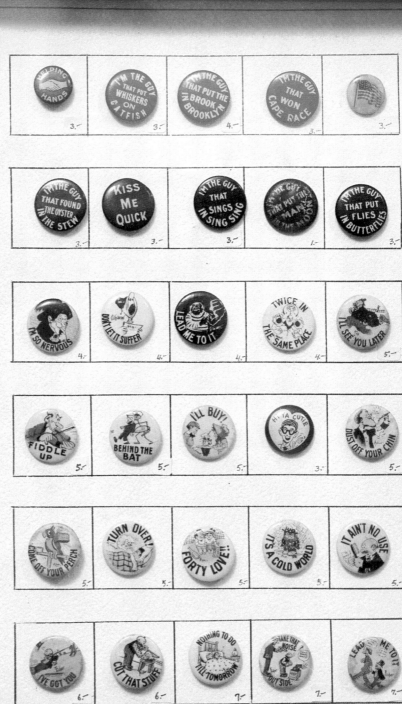

# Fabric Designers

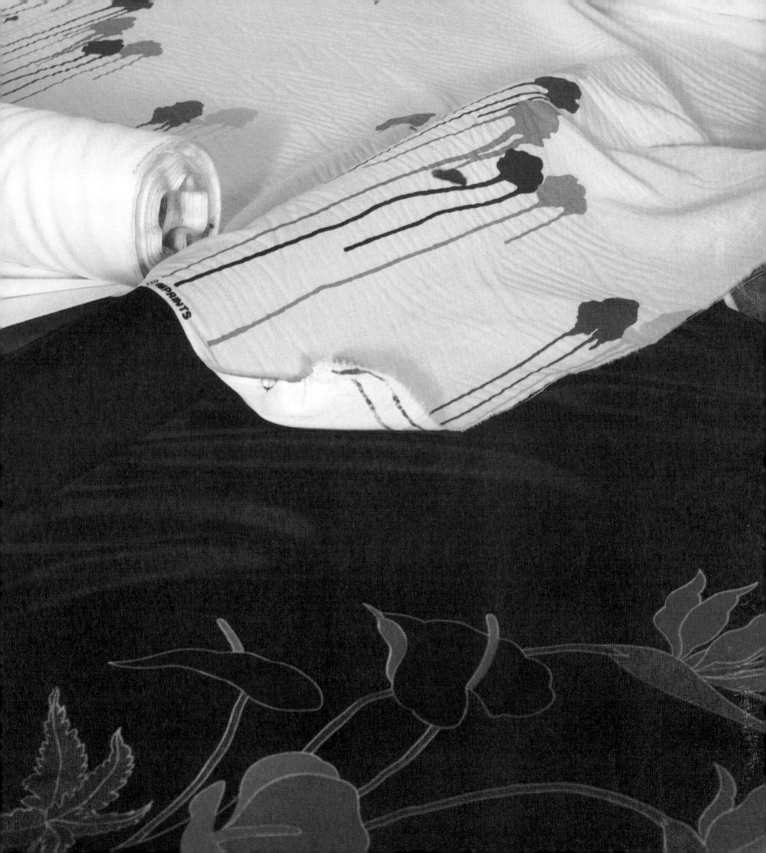

# A Theater Manager

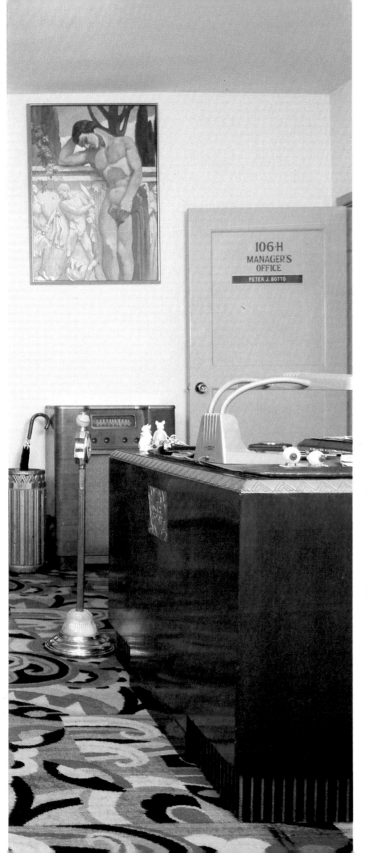

# A Clothing Designer